"What sets Shaye's poetry collection apart is the series of accompanying essays exploring each poem in greater detail. A tactic that...actually proves quite charming."

~Kirkus Indie Reviews

Publication Information Page

Copyright © 2013 Jasmynne Shaye

All rights reserved.
New York, NY

Published by Tasty Chuckle Publications
P.O. Box 48623
Cumberland, North Carolina 28331

Printed in the United States of America. All rights reserved under International Copyright Law. Contents and/or cover may not be reproduced in whole or in part in any form without expressed written consent of the publisher.

Still Standing logo created by OneSixFiveDesigns. Front cover designed by Imaginative Reality.

For more information on Jasmynne Shaye, please visit: www.jasmynneshaye.com.

ISBN: 0615909191
ISBN 13: 9780615909196

Dedication

This book is dedicated to all those who have been knocked down once or more in life. My message to you is that your past does not dictate your future, and no matter how ugly the situation is, there's always a way out. You may not see it right this second, today, or even tomorrow, but I promise you, it's there. Stay positive and hopeful that things will change for the better, and keep your eyes and heart focused on those things that bring you joy. Yes, it's easier said than done, but as you turn these pages, think about how to pick yourself up, dust yourself off, and get back on your path to success. It is very possible and it is very doable.

With love and encouragement,
Jasmynne Shaye

Still Standing

Jasmynne Shaye

Depth Perception, your presence will be forever missed.

Acknowledgments

Still Standing isn't just a book or the title of a poem, it's who I am. And I'm not sure how or where to begin to thank those who have helped me become the person I am today, but I will do my very best to try.

Thank you, God, for keeping me safe. I realize I could have, and maybe should have, been taken from this earth a long time ago, but You chose to save me and I am forever grateful. To my mother and father I say, "Thank you." Though we've not always seen eye to eye, I thank both of you for everything you've done for me. I don't take any of it for granted.

Thank you to the family I created in Los Angeles. You all kept me motivated and encouraged at all times, and you helped me realize my purpose. Thank you to my biological family for always supporting me from afar.

I need to give a bit of special gratitude to a few key individuals who helped bring this project together: Spencer Owens, Jaimyon Parker, and Hustle Diva. And a special thank you to Poetically Speaking and Urban Legends for giving me a platform to share my work.

Last, but certainly not least, I want to say thank you to all the friends and mentors who filled me with tiny nuggets of wisdom through the years. Whether I know you personally or you're only a friend in my head, there is no doubt that I would have been a crazy person long ago if not for the example you set, coupled with your guidance and encouragement. Thank you to anyone who has ever said a prayer for me, lent me their ear, or given me a smile. All were well-timed and appreciated beyond measure.

Foreword

Jasmynne Shaye, born and raised in Wilmington, North Carolina, is an American actor, poet, writer, and business owner. She began her career in the performing arts as a dancer, but while matriculating at North Carolina State University, Ms. Shaye recognized she could give a voice to all her gifts and talents. That burning desire felt by most great artists such as Maya Angelou, Oprah Winfrey, and Natasha Trethewey led her to the bright lights of Hollywood. Once the desire became all encompassing, Jasmynne loaded up her car and drove across country to lend a voice to the voiceless, expression to the expressionless, and to instill hope, passion, courage, and vigor in any and every audience she was blessed to stand before. Once in Hollywood, Ms. Shaye's talents were recognized immediately and she was hired to perform in shows, poetry slams, web series, and films.

While working in the entertainment industry in Hollywood, I was asked by the director to stand beside a talented actor who had the poise of a queen, skin of a goddess, and hair from a fairytale. After action was called, I was unable to speak my lines due to the magnetic and radiant energy that was coming from beside me. From that day forward I have been an active follower of the life and actions of Jasmynne Shaye. In May 2009, she debuted her one-woman show titled "Stepping on a Few Toes" to sold-out audiences all over Los

Angeles. I was in the audience opening night but did not get a chance to speak to the show-stopping, crowd-pleasing, emotion-conjuring Shaye because every audience member, tears in their eyes, begged for a moment of her time, thanking her for not only sharing her story, but for sharing theirs as well. I stood back in awe and admiration as I secretly wiped tears from my own eyes—not just at the story and performance, but at the privilege of seeing a star, humanitarian, and world changer right before my eyes in one singular person. The show led to award nominations, rave performance reviews in L.A.'s top publications, and waves of followers, supporters, and fans.

This book of poetry digs deep into the soul and nature of every individual. It serves as inspiration to the bowed-headed, light to the darkened paths, and hope to those who are on the brink of giving up. We all experience times when we feel we cannot go any further, but all we need is a push to take that next winning step. *Still Standing* is your push. Jasmynne's story is your story, your best friend's story, and even my story. She gives a voice to the heart's dearest cries and victories. From the South to the West Coast and now the East, Ms. Shaye is being seen, heard, and applauded for her honesty, dedication to her craft, and leaving her emotions on the page so that all her fans can experience their moment of invincibility and empowerment. A Southern belle with the talent of a Hollywood star and the gift of a poet laureate, I introduce to you: Jasmynne Shaye.

Justin Key
Actor | Speaker | Model
www.justindkey.com

Table of Contents

Multidimensional	1
Invisible	4
A Wish	8
My Favorite Book	12
Fast Asleep	16
Be Mine	20
Best Friend	23
Just as Bad	26
Blue Moment	31
I Have	35
Family Ties	39
How Do You Write a Poem?	44

In Spite of You 49

Nothing on Paper 53

Still Standing 57

Introduction

This book is the companion piece to my poetry CD of the same title. It contains five additional poems not included on the CD, as well as accompanying narratives called *A Closer Look*. Many of these poems were written as far back as 2003, and though I recall why each one was written and the purpose it served me at the time, *A Closer Look* isn't the place for that discussion. Instead these narratives are meant to be messages of hope and encouragement inspired by the accompanying poem. Wherever you are, whatever you're doing…I want you to read closely and enjoy *Still Standing*.

To obtain a copy of the *Still Standing* CD, please visit www.jasmynneshaye.com.

Multidimensional

Waiting on the cusp of forever and eternity.
Running to the border of smiles and hilarity.
Searching for the division of sadness and tears.
Digging to find the separation of loneliness and solitude.
Dancing on the endpoints of embarrassment and shame.
Climbing to the edge of excitement and thrill.
Crawling around the corner of empathy and politeness.
Stopping at the brink of fright and fear.
And that was just today.

• • •

A Closer Look: "Multidimensional"

No matter how cool someone presents themselves as or tries to be, if he is human, he feels feelings. They're involuntary reactions to external stimuli. They are flavored by your past experiences and enhanced by what you hope the future holds. Somewhere along the way, you were taught that visible feelings were a sign of weakness, and with each passing year, men and women alike work harder and harder to appear unbothered, unchanged, and unaffected. But I would argue that's about the silliest bit of behavior a person can exhibit. If that were so right and so perfect, you'd never hold babies. You would never kiss them. You would never rock them in your lap, and you would most certainly never engage in baby talk with them.

The same goes for your domesticated pets. If we more-evolved humans didn't show feelings and emotions, there would never be a need to cuddle with a cat, take a nap with a dog, or let either of them lick your face. But we've gone so far as to coin the term "pet person" so that we can accurately describe such behavior with ease. You love your pets, and whether you verbalize it or not, your heart beams with pride and joy each time you enter your home and get that special greeting from them. They're always excited to see you and they don't mind showing it. And allow me to call a spade a spade: you love it.

You love your pets; you love lunching with your friends, playing ball with the boys, shopping with the girls, and date nights with your sig fig. Even those of you who love your solitude (me included) crave opportunities to bond with those who are special to you. Come on, you're human! We weren't meant to exist alone, and none of us would want to. We want each other and we need each other. Human interaction feeds the soul, and you desire it just as you desire anything else. It just so happens that some choose not to show it, and all I ask is that you be patient with them. You've heard it before, but it's worth repeating: it's often the ones with the toughest exteriors who have the softest interiors. What you'll typically find is that life's challenges have hardened them and that thick exoskeleton is only there to protect them. And believe you me, they are secretly praying you'll have the patience to chip away at it bit by bit, because they feel things too. Laughter, tears, happiness, fright, thrill…we've all been there. We're all multidimensional. Your neighbor is no different from you, no matter their zip code, no matter their income. Feelings don't discriminate. Remember that the next time you're puzzled by someone's behavior. You have no idea what she may be dealing with. And for that person in your life who just won't open up, be patient. An oyster's shell may be tough, but look what it's holding inside.

We're all multidimensional.

Invisible

Through the water—
Through the glass—
No reflection in the mirror—
Lifted fog.

I spoke—I even smiled.
I chuckled at his jokes,
Even when they weren't that funny.
I patted his back when all others wouldn't.
I live to hear his thoughts.
I long to see his smile.
I crave his laughter.
I yearn for his touch.
I ache for his shoulder.
I wish he ached for mine.

His words excite me.
His walk reminds me of a solitary dove flying high.

But I am the topcoat.
I am the man without a face.
I am his dog's barrier.

His stare melts me,

And his lips I want to kiss.
I want to be the tail to his head.

His laughter is contagious.
His strength dissolves my fear.
He undresses me completely.
His conversations unzip my soul.
His touch unbuttons my heart.
His humanity unclasps my generosity.

I hear him daily in my thoughts.
I see him nightly in my dreams.
Yet I am air.
He does not see me.
I am invisible.

• • •

A Closer Look: "Invisible"

Whether you know it or not, someone is always watching.

Sure, there may be times when you feel like no matter what you do, you just can't seem to get the attention of a certain someone, but remember this—only you can make you feel invisible. Everywhere you go and with everything you do, you're being watched and noticed by someone. That realization alone should get you excited, because it encourages you to always put your best foot forward. Think about it: no matter where you go, no matter what you're doing, someone is always taking notice. Perhaps I'm the only one, but I think that's a pretty big deal. Someone is always looking at you, and it's up to you to impress or underwhelm. And how about this for a twist of lime: even though you think that certain someone can't see you, they're totally watching. Now you should really perk up and take note, because there are a couple take-aways I want you to leave with. The first is integrity and the second is confidence.

I've heard it stated that integrity is who you are when no one is looking. I love that statement and I think of it quite often. When you don't think you've got an audience, when you don't think you're on camera, when you don't think a soul can see you, how do you behave? You in those moments are so telling and so revealing. But understand that you've got all the control. You can choose to litter or put your garbage in the proper receptacle. You can choose to have road rage or to be kind to your neighbor in traffic. Every day you're faced with these kinds of choices, and every day is comprised of a series of decisions. Each decision holds a piece of the puzzle to your character; all the while, you are determining who you want to be. That's integrity.

Confidence is where it gets exciting. You want my two cents on getting noticed by that special someone? Be you. Be you 100 percent. Don't be who you think you should be or who you think that person wants you to be. Just. Be. You. Here's the kicker: confidence is magnetic, and there is nothing more attractive and charismatic than a confident person. Confidence is that intangible thing that makes you smile when you see someone from afar. It's a bit of flare that only you have, so exercise it and use it to your benefit. Stop stressing about whether the person is looking—trust me, they are. Question is, what message are you sending? One of deceit and fear, or one of integrity and confidence? Use your time wisely and make the right choices—every day.

A Wish

Wishing I was holding you…
Wishing you were here right now, or wishing I was there.
Wishing we were breathing from the same supply of air.
Wishing we were having some kind of secret love affair.
Wishing your eyes would catch me with that penetrating, intimate stare.
Wishing I was running my fingers through your charming hair.
But none of this has happened,
So I'll continue to hope, and say a little prayer…
Wishing, wishing…wishing.
Wishing I could find the words to say how much I care.

• • •

A Closer Look: "A Wish"

Raise your hand if you've ever had someone tell you on the last day of school that they've had a crush on you all year. I know I'm not the only one out there with yearbooks filled with cute love notes from those who chose to admire from afar. As flattering as that is, your response is always the same: "Why didn't you say something?!?" At the time, you may have received any number of answers to that question, but I'm willing to bet money that at some point the tables turned, transferring that scaredy-cat energy to you. And I'll bet you've sung the "But This Is Different" song more times than you can count.

So what's the deal? Why does the cat always seem to get your tongue when you're trying to muster the strength to approach someone romantically or even just pay them a compliment? That simple act turns Chatty Cathys into Mousy Marthas, and Macho Marks into Timid Tonys in a second. A number of guys have told me that approaching women is no easy task, and even though I hear them, I don't quite understand. Perhaps because I work in the entertainment industry, my once-baby-soft skin has been replaced with tough elephant hide. In my line of work, you're constantly being judged and rejected. It comes with the territory, so the word "no" doesn't bother me as much. And I'd love for you to get to the place where you become less concerned with it as well. It's all in your perception, expectations, attitude, and delivery.

Let's get started.

If you perceive the situation as a difficult one, then it will be. So the first thing you have to do is change your mindset. Instead of, "Oh my gosh, how am I gonna do this?," say, "This is a piece of cake. There's nothing to be afraid of." Then, I want you to shift your expectations. Whatever the message is that you want to express, do so without expecting anything in return. Don't go into it praying to receive a response in kind, because the person doesn't have to give you one. If that's your motivation, get rid of it. That reeks of "Do you like me? Check one: yes or no," and that's not the game you want to be involved in. That's not what this is about. Asserting yourself in this manner is about learning to fully express yourself and being comfortable in your own skin. It's about overcoming fear and regaining your confidence. I'll even go one step further. Have you forgotten what Mark Twain said? "I can live for two months on a good compliment." How about you think of your message as a gift you're giving—again, expecting nothing in return.

"That color really brings out your eyes."

"I like your new haircut."

"You look amazing in that dress."

"What are you wearing? Your cologne smells great."

"Those jeans were made for you."

"You're incredibly handsome."

Think of giving those compliments as gifts. All of a sudden you have the opportunity to bring joy to another and put a smile on someone's face. Where's the fear in that? What's there to be afraid of?

Quite the opposite, don't you think? You should be ecstatic. There's your attitude adjustment. And when you deliver your gift—whatever the message is—do so with humility and sweet kindness. There's no need to call attention to yourself or to the situation, so lower your voice. This isn't something that needs to be yelled across the room or announced on the loudspeaker. It's a personal message, so deliver it personally—not through a friend or a friend of a friend. Deliver it with a smile on your face, and if the circumstance doesn't allow for conversation, a note will do. Once you've given your gift, smile and walk away. Your job has been done. It's really that easy, and you've now changed the situation in such a way that rejection has been removed from the equation entirely. You're not baring your soul and you're not sharing the deepest emotions of your heart. You're giving a compliment—nothing more, nothing less. And what you'll find is that when you put this kind of energy out, it always comes back to you, which will act as fuel to your fire. Pretty soon you'll look in the mirror and won't remember when or how you became so confident, and it won't even matter. Ride the wave and reap the benefits, because confidence will take you where you want to go when skill and talent are unable to get you on the guest list.

My Favorite Book

I hear his emotions…

I understand his fear.
I comprehend his sadness.
I've experienced his anger.
I've dealt with his insecurities.
I've swallowed his hurt.
I've dreamt his nightmares.
I've sat with his solitude.

I've seen life through his eyes.
I've walked the path in his shoes.
I've cried over his spilled milk.
I am he, and he is me.
And I love him,
Because he, too, is multidimensional;
As complicated as a Rubik's Cube.

But you were too foolish to open the book.
You, like everyone else, judged him by his cover.
True enough, it had no colorful photographs,
And no exciting captions,
But I opened the pages anyway.
And as a result—

He whispered passion.
He spoke of desire.
He acted with courage.
He illustrated delight.
He yelled excitement.
He exemplified drive.
He personified determination.

I have read his text,
And he is now—my favorite book.

· · ·

A Closer Look:
"My Favorite Book"

It's been said a swillion times: "Never judge a book by its cover." Yet you do it anyway. At first glance, you have immediate thoughts about everyone you see.

The girl whose bare skin is hidden under a blanket of tattoos...

The Sikh wearing the turban...

The teen girl carrying a baby...

The man in the business suit...

The girl who, as best you can tell, has had everything pierced—twice...

The guy who looks like he's never cut his beard a day in his life...

The nun in her habit...

The teen boy wearing a hoodie...

The cleaning lady at Holiday Inn...

The guy with his earlobes stretched so much you could fit several fingers through them…

The obese girl at McDonald's…

The effeminate boy in your math class…

The doorman at Trump Tower…

You get the picture. Week in and week out, you see these people. Most of them you will never so much as say hello to, all the while jumping to conclusions about who they are, what they eat, and what they do in their spare time. I do understand that a little bit of prejudice is human nature, but I don't want you to let it be your knee-jerk reaction every single time. I want you to get to the place where it no longer clouds your views of other human beings. Truth be told, if you took a minute to have a real conversation with the guy that has the insanely long dreadlocks, you'd find that the two of you aren't all that different. Perhaps you both have children and are both equally concerned about the quality of education and the school system in your area. Or maybe he's into fitness too, and is currently training for the marathon you've been thinking of running. Maybe he's an attorney who can give you some words of wisdom before you head off to law school. Whatever the situation, chances are the two of you have much more in common than you think—and that can be said for most. I learned a long time ago to be open in that way, and I'm glad I did, because it's led to some memorable encounters and some very special friendships. It doesn't hurt to give another the time of day. If you find them not to be your cup of tea, move on—but there's definitely no way of telling without first being cordial. Leave the judging to Judy. It's her job, she's good at it, plus it frees up your time for other things…like finding your favorite book.

Fast Asleep

running from regret
slowly.
leaving mediocrity behind
while holding its hand.
peeking into the future
blinded.
laughing with my husband
with no voice.
picking lilac flowers
with no hands.
watching the sunrise
at midnight.
writing a best-seller
with no pen.
planting an apple tree
on cement.
picking out constellations
in daylight.
making her dreams come true
with incompetence.
crossing the finish line
at the starting gate.
crying at their weddings
with dry eyes.

dancing on stage
behind closed doors.
painting the basement walls
with no brush.
submerging into joy
ascended.
providing for those that don't have
starving.
wearing only the best
naked.
photographing perfection
with no film.
loving unconditionally
like the wind.
fishing at the lake
in the desert.
camping in the wilderness
with electricity.
walking in confidence and pride
ashamed.
driving the finest of all
hitchhiking.
standing for truth and honesty
liar.
leaving a legacy of strength
broken.
following the path according to plan
confused.
seeing everything so clear
in the fog.
i'm dreaming.

• • •

A Closer Look: "Fast Asleep"

One of the hardest things in the world to do is turn your thoughts, dreams, and ambitions into reality. It's hard as hell. As a kid, you have gargantuan dreams of all kinds. They change like the wind and you confidently share them with everyone.

"I'm gonna be president!"

"When I grow up, I'm gonna drive a fast motorcycle."

"I want to be the best guitar player in the world."

"Watch—I'm going to be the best clothing designer you have ever seen."

And the list goes on. You want to be painters and singers; you want to sail around the world; and you want to rise to fame in your favorite sport. As a kid you want it all, and you are naïve enough to believe you can have it.

Then time passes. Age falls upon you and you're taught the phrase "Be realistic." So those of you who believe you had your head in the clouds slowly float back down to earth in an effort to achieve realism…but you don't stop dreaming. Your mind won't let you stop. And so you sit, stuck in your today while frantically reaching for the tomorrows in your head. And that's a tough place to be. Oftentimes your today directly contradicts the tomorrows you yearn for, and you haven't the first clue how to change that. Single people ache to be married. The jobless dream of employment. The childless pray that they'll one day be saddled with dirty diapers. Those without legs wish to run marathons, and the poor dream of wealth. Likewise, scholars dream of being entrepreneurs. Collegiate athletes pray they'll go pro. High-school teachers talk of becoming university professors. Home cooks daydream about becoming professional chefs, and garage bands have their fingers and toes crossed that their music will one day be played on the radio. Dreaming is intuitive. No one has to tell you to do it or give you instructions on how it's done. It's a map that was imprinted on your brain before you were able to speak discernible words. Even still, with all those years of practice, it is very difficult to connect the dots. Most will go to their graves never having done so because it's just that challenging.

So why bother? Well, because whether asleep or awake, your dreams give you hope. You've just got to put procrastination to bed and master the art of following through. Once you spit in the face of fear and give yourself a pep talk, there really isn't much you can't accomplish. So please, never put your dreams to rest. Never belittle them, because they are who you are on your best day, and it's up to you to take the steps to bring those visions to fruition.

Be Mine

I need you to hug me like I'm all that exists.
I need you to hold my hand because it draws us closer.
I need you to smile when you see me because my presence excites you!
I need you to brag about my accomplishments to your friends.
I need you to miss me when we haven't talked in a while.
I need you to fight my battles for me.
I need you to care for me when I'm ill, because you would have it no other way.
I need you to call me first thing because that bit of conversation is just what you need to get your day off to a good start.
I need you to encourage me because your happiness is tied to my success.
I need you to ask me twenty questions because you want to know every detail.
I need you to laugh with me because when we chuckle in unison—well, it just doesn't get any better.
I need you to kiss my forehead.
I need you to hold me tight.
I need you to love me.
I need you to be my mother.

• • •

A Closer Look:
"Be Mine"

Mothers are the original best friends.

That's not said to take anything away from all the amazing fathers out there, but for the vast majority of you, your mother carried you for nine months and was the first to hold you when you were born. And for the mothers who nursed, the bonds created were that much stronger. For the first several months of your life, your mother was your lifeline. Whether your father was there or not, there's no mistaking the connection between mother and child. It's indescribable. But as time marches on, classmates and friends begin to occupy the space once reserved for Mom. Your priorities change and fluctuate so much that you become unrecognizable to your mother at times. And even during the most difficult of years, when all the two of you seem to do is butt heads, your love for her is unwavering. You may raise your voice, stomp your feet, and call her names, but you would never want any harm to come to her. That's your mother.

Now, to all the moms…I don't think anyone can be quoted as saying parenting is easy. Everyone knows it's the toughest job a man or woman will ever have. Even with all the books and online tools at your fingertips, maneuvering through the day-to-day intricacies of it all is more than challenging. But if I can plead for every child out there, parents, please never give up on your kids. Please never throw the towel in. Please never surrender to the trials; do all you can to overcome them. Your children are counting on you. They may throw a fit and act a fool, but they appreciate the rules you set. Your allowing them to do any and every thing sends a message that you don't care. They want you to care about their grades. They want you to be interested in their friends and whom they're dating. They love it when you ask questions about them. All of these things send messages of care and concern, and that's what everyone wants and needs from their mother.

And moms, if you yourself came from a broken home or a family drenched in dysfunction, vow to break the cycle. The moment you become pregnant, you are given an enormous amount of power, and you've got some pretty hefty choices to make. Will you continue on as your mother and grandmother did, or will you forge a new path? Never mind the material things. That newborn baby won't care one bit about the brand name on the side of his crib or what tag is in the back of her onesie. All babies care about is the love you shower them with, the hugs you share, and the memories you create. Parenting is absolutely the toughest job you will ever have, but when done right, the rewards are plentiful. You can step back and smile with pride because you know you went above and beyond to shape and mold your child into an extraordinary human being. And believe me, she loves you for it.

Best Friend

It's bringing sunshine to my rain.
It's knowing my hurt and feeling my pain.
Always listening when I call your name.
It's being my best friend.

It's always answering when I call.
It's helping me up each time I fall.
Giving me a push when I hit the wall.
It's being my best friend.

At the last minute, changing your plans.
Sitting with me, holding my hand.
Continuing to say, "Bug, you can!"
It's being my best friend.

Many will always come and go.
Few will stick, this, I know.
I love you more than I can show.
You are my best friend.

• • •

A Closer Look: "Best Friend"

You all have schoolmates, classmates, associates, buddies, co-workers, and colleagues. For the most part, they put smiles on your face and they're cool peeps to hang out with from time to time. But there's no one like your ace. Those one or two special folks you wouldn't trade for all the gold in the world. They've been there with you through thick and thin. You've cried on their shoulder and they've cried on yours. The moment you met, there was an instant click, as if you were cut from the same cloth. You finished each other's sentences and laughed together like you'd known each other for years. There's no way to forecast what's to come next, but you knew right away that this was a person you absolutely wanted to spend more time with and get to know better. Slowly but surely time ticks away, and before you know it, the two of you are referring to each other as best friends.

Thank God for them, right? What on earth would you do without their listening ear and their voice of reason? On a good day, your bestie pushes you to be more than you are; on a bad day they veg out with you as you lick your wounds—and even that's welcome because you're doing it together.

I'm talking about camaraderie. It's one of those necessary intangibles that not only keeps you smiling, it also keeps you from pulling the last of your hair out. I won't be the first or the last to say it, but you can't choose your family. Your parents, siblings, and cousins were given to you by blood, but your friends you get to hand-select. As a kid you don't really pay much attention to it. You're friends with the kids on the playground, with the girls in dance class, and with the guys on the team. But as you mature, your priorities, needs, and wants change. As the years go by, you may shed skin like a snake—almost reinventing yourself, always striving to be the best you that you can be. And as you journey along, becoming more like the person you believe you were meant to be, I urge you to also become more selective with the friends you make. This is in no way meant to slight anyone, but why wouldn't you want to be a bit more selective? You should always want to keep people around you who sincerely have your best interests at heart. People who will motivate you, inspire you, and encourage you at all times. But you also want them to be able to keep it real with you—to be able to tell you when you're not behaving as you should and help you get back on track. Be careful that you're not outgrowing your friends and senselessly holding on to them because you're too afraid to let go. I'm sure to some of you it sounds like I'm double-talking my face off right now, as I just said that BFFs are worth their weight in gold, and now I'm suggesting that you drop them like a bad habit. No. That's not my message at all. I just want you to be cautious. You may never reach this point, but if you get to a place where you and your bestie just don't seem to "fit" right any longer, it may be time to move on. I'm giving you the go-ahead to do so. It's OK. No matter how strong the bond once was, friendships do end from time to time, often as a result of personal growth. Unfortunately, if the two of you aren't growing at the same pace or in the same direction, it can cause strain that feels like a flashing red light letting you know that things must come to an end. Please, never feel bad when this happens, because even this is a necessary part of life. In the meantime, enjoy your besties while you have them. I know they mean the world to you, because mine mean the world to me.

Just as Bad

How many times have I said...

People get on my nerves!
Why don't people just leave well enough alone?
I wish people weren't so two-faced.
People need to stop being so judgmental.
People should learn to forgive and forget.
When will people stop frontin'?
People around here got small minds and need to think bigger.
People need to show love to their kids.
Why aren't people more polite?
People just need to grow up!!
I 'clare I wish I had a dollar for all the times people asked to touch my hair.
No sense in holdin' back. People need to just say what they feel.
People need to stop obsessing over the American standard of beauty and be happy with self.
Why don't people grow a backbone and stop giving in to every temptation that blows their way?
People need to quit stallin' and tell that guy or girl how they feel. He or she may not always be available.
How 'bout it's time for people to figure out that it ain't always cool to be cool.

I am so sick of people thinkin' every brotha with a 'fro want they money.
People need to realize it's OK to cry.
People need to quit tellin' all they business to anyone who will listen.
When will people realize there is no middle of the road? It's either right or wrong.
I really wish people would stop trying to be cute.
How 'bout just let me know when people start using condoms on a consistent basis.
I've been ready for people to accept the fact that there is only one way to Heaven. It takes a little more than being a good person.
I will be SO glad when more people start to take responsibility for their own actions.
Why don't people clean up what they mess up?
When will people figure out the meaning of "till death do us part"?
How 'bout even though Milton Bradley want us to believe otherwise, people need to understand that LIFE is not a game.
People need to stop lettin' they twelve-year-old daughters dress like they seventeen. But then again… the apple probably doesn't fall far from the tree.
People need not be afraid to follow their dreams.
People need to stop thinkin' every Middle Easterner is a terrorist.
The time is long overdue for people to realize emotions are not to be played with.

I used to just want to lock myself in a room and get away from people altogether, until
I opened the door, let someone in, and realized…
I am people too.

· · ·

A Closer Look: "Just as Bad"

OMG. Don't you hate when someone cuts you off in traffic, or won't let you merge onto the freeway? Or when you're exiting a building directly behind someone and they let the door slam in your face? You weren't asking them to lay their jacket over a puddle for you, but it would have been nice not to have the door knock you in the nose. I hate to hear elementary school kids use profanity. Oh my goodness, I hate it when people are passive-aggressive! Isn't that annoying? They're upset with you but they're not man or woman enough to tell you straight up. Instead they pout and whimper, waiting for you to guess what's ailing them. Irks me to no end. What about bandwagoners? Don't you hate them too? The folks who don't seem to have any true ideas or opinions of their own? You know the ones. They like what's hot when it's hot but don't stick with any one thing for too long. They quickly move on to the next craze just as soon as the Kardashians announce what it is. What about the fakers? Don't you hate them too? The ones who want to be liked and accepted so badly that they create these elaborate back stories for themselves?—completely false stories, of course. Their need to be a part of something trumps their desire to be authentic.

I'll bet you could spend all day talking about the ways people work your nerves, and the things they do that make you want to escape to solitude. There is no shortage of things that grind your gears (to borrow a line from *Family Guy*). So how do you cope? How do you get on with your life, moving from day to day with all these things constantly getting under your skin? I'll give you two ways. First, have a little compassion. Second, take a look in the mirror.

Let's tackle compassion first. Call me naïve, but I like to believe that people are mostly good. And even good people have bad days and act out from time to time. When that person cut you off in traffic, he could have been being a jerk just for the sake of it—sure, that's always a possibility. But it's also very possible he was on his way to a friend in need, or to tend to an urgent family matter. When the person ahead of you let the door slam in your face, I'll bet she didn't even realize you were back there. Chances are she had zoned out and her thoughts were elsewhere—perhaps prepping for the job interview she was headed to, or planning that evening's dinner in her mind. It really could have been anything. As for the fakers…well, even they could use a little compassion. At the end of the day, they just want to be accepted. For whatever reason, they fear you won't like the real them, so they do their best to please you. Almost like every employee on their first day of work at a new company, making every effort to put their best foot forward. It almost makes sense, right? What you'll find is that when you show even just a smidge of compassion to these folks, it keeps you from being a big ball of tension and anger. You can let go of the road rage and the tit-for-tat mentality of praying that the universe gives them theirs. Instead, reach down within yourself and assume the best. Assume their senseless behavior was unintentional so that you can go on with your day without the negative energy that those interactions typically cause. You just don't need it. Besides, you don't want to be that person retelling the story (over and over) of how someone stole your parking space. You're better than that.

Which brings me to this business of taking a look in the mirror. Simply put, none of us is perfect. Each of us has flaws and -isms that don't sit well with others. On any given day, you could be that person working someone else's nerves without even knowing it. Trust me, it happens. And the sooner you realize that, the easier it becomes to show compassion to your neighbor, because like it or not, we've all worn their shoes at one time or another.

Blue Moment

shades of sadness—
hues of laughter—
textures of gladness—
then and here after.

colors of shame—
positions of anger—
slices of blame—
but never felt danger.

flavors of care—
spices of home—
glimmers of flare—
but now you're gone.

buckets of retreat—
volumes of safety—
slivers of deceit—
i'm missing you lately.

shadows of heat—
dots of strife—
plates of strength—
still took your life.

JASMYNNE SHAYE

future for children—
plans for two—
your memory will know them—
but they won't know you.

• • •

A Closer Look: "Blue Moment"

Death, unfortunately, is a very natural part of life, but sometimes life deals you a hard one and a friend or loved one is gone too soon. Whether it's a parent, grandparent, child, cousin, or dear friend, the pain is the same and it hurts like hell. You miss them like crazy and your brain is flooded with images of days gone by. Memories of them laughing and smiling dance in your thoughts. You might even get attacked by a little regret, wishing you'd spent more time with them, kicking yourself for not telling them how awesome you thought they were. And as time drifts on, the memories become less vivid as the images in your mind begin to cloud, and even this is upsetting. You loved this person, but now you're finding it hard to picture their face. Don't beat yourself up about it. It happens to the best of us, and there's not a whole lot you can do about it, but this is my two cents: love them while they're here, and take lots of pictures.

Today everyone's phone is a camera, but don't think it's only for the tweens. I would argue that everyone should be taking a page out of their book. Yes, it can get a tad silly if you're Instagramming every minutia of your life, but there's something to cataloging special moments with special people. There will come a time when you will be scrolling back through your social media feed, smiling happily because you've captured those timeless moments on film. And for those who are anti-FaceTwittaGram, snap your pics and head to the nearest drugstore to print your hard copies. Yes. You can still do that. I get picked on all the time for being camera-happy, but do you think I care? I know that I'm capturing memories for my personal safekeeping, and that gets me excited.

And this is a stern message to everyone reading this page: make time to let those important to you know how much you care. Perhaps it's a monthly phone call, email, lunch date, or a bit of snail mail (that, too, is still a thing). However you choose to show your love, do it with sincerity and it will be well-received each and every time. Call it hokey, but don't call it pointless. Don't even take my word for it; try it for yourself. Out of the blue, send someone a heartfelt email letting them know how much they mean to you and watch the response you get. Believe me, it's worth it. Go back and reread "Blue Moment" if you need a reminder, but there will come a time when that person is no longer here. Don't wish you had done something different. Do something different now.

I Have

Do you ever feel this way?

Ever want to be ugly for just one day?
Ever get tired of being touched that way?
Knowing exactly what he will say…
To get you to stay. To get you to lay.
Knowing with every kiss there's a price you must pay.

Looking in the mirror, and hating what you see.
Asking continually, "Can this really be me?"
Wondering if one day you will ever be free
From the constant, persistent, never-ending agony.
But you have lived the alternative, and have been lonely.
"This has to be more fun than that could ever be!"

Ashamed of your sight.
About to lose your fight.
Always giving in; never standing upright.

Wanting to undo the past to erase the hurt and pain.
Wanting for all the sins to get washed away by the rain.

Please don't touch me anymore.
Don't ask for one more kiss.

Let me go when I want to leave;
Don't grab me on the wrist.

Please don't smile 'cause you think I'm cute.
Don't wink when you pass me by.
I'm telling you now, "I'm not in the mood."
So when I diss, you won't wonder why.

I'm taking it back from you, and reclaiming my body,
Reclaiming my dignity and pride.
Ask again for a late night visit,
And trust—you will be denied.

I want to look in the mirror and like what I see.
I want to find out exactly what it means to be me.
I want to see my reflection and be forced to smile.
I realize this change may take a little while.

But I am ready, and I will commit,
The journey may be long, but I know I'll make it.
No matter how tough, I promise not to quit,
Until the goal is reached and I can admit

That I'm a new person, renewed from within.
Focused on tomorrow, not thinking 'bout where I've been.

Excited to live each and every day,
No matter the circumstance, sunshine or gray.
They will never again take this away.
Never to sway. Never to stray.

Do you ever feel this way?

• • •

A Closer Look: "I Have"

I'm going to talk to the ladies for a minute....Men, feel free to share this message with the women in your lives.

Girls…women…ladies. Hear me when I say this: you have all the power. For the most part, no man (or other human being, for that matter) can belittle you, take advantage of you, or abuse you without your consent. No one. Only you can give a person the green light to mistreat you. To use a phrase from the streets, if you "man up" and stiffen your spine, it sends a message of strength and confidence to all those around you, and that's the message you want to send. This next bit may not be for everybody, but I know it's for somebody, so I'm going to proceed. This business of staying in abusive relationships has got to stop, and it's got to stop now. If there are children present, you're sending them a destructive message that may take years to undo. I'll leave it to someone else to school the men on their reckless behavior. For now I want to speak loud and clear to my ladies. You are not a punching bag. You are not a sex slave. You are not a doormat. You are a beautiful being capable of bringing another life into this world, and you are worth much more than you give yourself credit for. Stop shortchanging yourself. Demand the respect you deserve, and demand it from everyone you meet.

To those who come from homes so broken you've never experienced love in a healthy way, or have never had a solid support system—I know it's hard. I'm not gonna lie to you, it's tough, but it's manageable. You don't have to settle for subpar relationships with men who want to steal your joy and everything else along with it. Be brave enough to love yourself. Have the courage to look in the mirror and encourage that person you see staring back at you, because for a while you may be your only cheerleader and I need you to be OK with that. Think of the daughter you have or hope to have someday. What kind of advice would you give to her? What pitfalls would you want to make certain she avoids? If she were taking notes on your every move, what kind of example would you want to set for her? Now be that. Learn to be the example for her whether she's looking or not, because in the end, it's really about you being kind to you. If you respect yourself, then by default, you force others to do the same.

And if you find yourself trapped in an unhealthy situation and you're uncertain how to get free, please speak to someone you feel you can trust. That's a weight I don't want you carrying by yourself. Seek the advice and assistance of someone who can help you devise a plan to get you on a path to restoration. Life is short and you deserve to experience the full joy of it while you're here. Think about all the smiles and laughter you're being cheated of and all the happy memories still to be created. Time is of the essence, and I don't want you wasting any more of it. Reclaim your power and bathe in the peace that follows, because you're worth it.

Family Ties

I love you more than words can say,
But that didn't seem to help that day...

It grabbed my throat—
It shook my knees—
I was engulfed by terror.
My thoughts raced a mile a minute
Looking for the error.

Why didn't I know?
What did I miss?
How could this pass me by?
Why didn't it show?
I know the list.
I know what it's like to cry.

I know what it's like to open a door,
And see nothing but empty space.
I know what it's like to crawl on the floor
Looking for that safe place.

Where you can sit for a minute,
And time stands still,
And every rose in in full bloom.

Where you can think for a second,
And not take the pill
You feel will erase your gloom.

Where you can hide for a lifetime,
And smile for a century,
Holding on to the good old days.
When life was fun—
One big jubilee—
Nothing like this melancholy phase.

"Do I really care?"
I have to ask myself;
Because I didn't see the signs.
Completely unaware—
Never took enough time
To read between the lines.

I look back now, and it was all there,
Just as plain as black and white.
I take the blame for being selfish.
My own problems clouded my sight.

Too concerned with me, mine, I.
Not nearly enough for him.
So bogged down with my own life,
Now the time we have is slim.

But I am dedicated to ensure
This story ends
Happily ever after.
I will do what I must,
And change my own habits
To hear your carefree laughter.

We have to lean on each other,
And get it all out.
Not hold things tight inside.
I am here for you—
You are my brother.
I want to give you what I was denied.

So call on me when
The darkness creeps in,
And you feel you have nowhere to turn.
I will answer, and do what I can,
Because your happiness is my main concern.

· · ·

A Closer Look:
"Family Ties"

For most, "family" is a touchy subject. Few are those fortunate enough to have had picture-perfect upbringings that resembled that of the Huxtables and the Cleavers. If ever there was a common denominator among humans, I believe family is it. Each and every one of us has a mother and a father. Whether we know them or not, biology tells us they both played a part in our creation. That's for all humans across the globe. No matter your race, ethnicity, religion, native tongue, socioeconomic status, or country of origin, everyone has a mother and father. And there is the beginning of family. That's where it starts. Not everyone has sisters and brothers. Not everyone has aunts and uncles or a multitude of cousins, but everyone has parents and grandparents. That's a point no one can argue. So, if only for the duration of this narrative, would you be so kind as to see everyone as equal just for a moment? As you're reading right now, understand that we're all the same. Everyone is someone's child. Everyone came from a mother and father, even in the case of artificial insemination. Though the father may be called a "donor," a man and woman were still involved in creating this new life. That's the beginning of it all—and some argue that's the end of it all too. In other words, at the end of the day, all you have is family. I'm sure you've heard that before. I pray each of you are able to lead full lives as healthy individuals, but should you end up in a hospital or nursing home later in life, who do you envision will be visiting you and tending to your care? Sure, there's a chance your classmates might stop by. A former coworker or two might pop in. But if you're being honest with yourself, it's your family that will be by your side most often. And it's your family that you'll want to see. You can argue with me on this point all you want, but you'll be wrong every single time. Even though you fight with them, call them names, and give them the silent treatment from time to time, you still love your family. In some cases it makes no logical sense, but that fact still remains.

I've said all this in an attempt to get you thinking outside yourself for a minute. There is no denying that life will happen, bringing you trials and tribulations that you'll have to sort through. You'll be slapped in the face with one family crisis after another. Whether someone is abusing drugs, gets arrested, is stricken with illness, faces teen pregnancy, abandons their children, or suffers a major accident, family will keep you stressed, worried, and on your toes at all times. Many of the mishaps will anger and upset you, leading you to want to disown the entire clan. But I'm going to ask you to pause for a moment. If you're able and if your mind will allow you to, think down the road ten, twenty, or thirty years. Picture those images that I described earlier. Remember your beginning, and, not to be morbid, but picture your ending. Family was all you had at the start of things, and there's a good chance they'll be all you have toward the end. So do what you can now to preserve those relationships. It's effort, it's work, and it's not always easy, as the ones you love the most tend to have the ability to cause you the most pain. But it's worth it. I was just at a nursing home visiting my great-uncle over the weekend, and though the environment was grim, my uncle wore a huge smile on his face because for the first time since becoming a resident, he had family by his side. I don't wish that situation on anyone, but as the years tick away, you're going to want blood to keep you company. So do the best you can now to foster those relationships. What you'll find is that the work is well worth the reward.

How Do You Write a Poem?

You have to get molested by your father's
Nephew, in the first grade, and
You have to hate him so much
That you can't even refer to him
As your cousin.

You have to tell your mother that
Her boyfriend is no good for her,
And is no good for her kids,
And have your mother say,
"But he helps me with the bills."

You have to feel like paying the rent
Is far more important
Than your family unit.

You have to take a sharp object
To your wrist.

You have to watch your mother
Whip your younger brother, and think,

"If she hits him one more time,
Surely he will pass out."

You have to hate your mother.

You have to be one of very few
Black people at a private white school,
And grow up thinking you're inferior.

You have to feel poor,
Even in your school uniform,
Because your navy blue pants
Aren't Outback Red.

You have to have your white "friends"
Laugh and pick at you, because
Your body isn't shaped like theirs.

You have to cry.

You have to get molested by your
Mother's boyfriend and tell no one.

You have to stand there yelling
As your father slaps your face
Hard enough to send your glasses airborne.

You have to smile when the
White girl on the playground says,
"We like you because you're not like most black people,"
Because you're too young to realize her ignorance.

You have to love no one.

You have to love anywhere
But home, and cherish those
Days, hours, minutes—
As the best moments in time.

You have to say good-bye to your roommate
Before you go to sleep, because
You just took many, many sleeping pills,
And you have to hate God when you wake up the next morning.

You have to let many guys
Lay on top of you,
Because you have become desensitized to sex,
And no longer see it as an act of love.

You have to hate yourself.

You have to love solitude.

You have to love your pen.

You have to live.

• • •

A Closer Look: "How Do You Write a Poem?"

I would argue that every artist of every kind has tasted a flavor of hardship in their lives, whether they're a singer, a dancer, a musician, a painter, an actor, a writer, or a comedian. If they are unmistakably phenomenal, and seem to pour their heart and soul into their work like none other, chances are they've been broken at some point and found a way to put the pieces of themselves back together again. And you know the ones I'm talking about. It's that dancer's performance that brings tears to your eyes. The singer whose voice gives you goose bumps. The musician who plays an instrument unfamiliar to you, but makes you stop in your tracks when you hear the mesmerizing sound. Who cares what the artist looks like and who cares where they're from; their talent comes from a place of raw, pure emotion and it speaks to all those that experience it. These people have been through something, and it has no choice but to come out in their work.

I am no different. It's challenging to be this transparent, but this poem speaks directly to the personal obstacles that I have had to overcome. I would never lie to you by saying the journey to healing has been an easy one, but it was absolutely a necessary one. If you don't choose a path of healing, the alternative for anyone dealing with muckety-muck is to remain an angry, toxic mess, destroying everything you touch. I had grown tired of that life and I desperately wanted something different. I had no clue how to heal my wounds, so early on I just did the best I could, seeming to make little or no headway at all. Admittedly, the -isms and phrases found on motivational posters weren't really helping me that much. I was too angry to think positively and my prayers just seemed to go unanswered, so I had to devise an alternative recipe for success. And without even knowing it, little by little I chipped away at my bitterness, putting out the fires of my pain and dissolving my depression. Without a doubt, I am not the person I used to be, and that's because I chose to be different, and I guess that's my message to you. It is impossible to erase the memory of whatever hell you've had to live through, but you don't have to let it rule your life and govern your future. Yes, it takes action and hard work on your part, but it is so worth it. When we allow those hurtful things to take us over, they destroy us physically, mentally, and emotionally. We become a fraction of ourselves, unable to experience all the goodness and joy that our lives have to offer. Instead we've let the dark cloud sit in the driver seat as we willingly go down whatever path it chooses take us. My call to you is: take your life back. Make the decision to send the clouds away so that you can be you again. Everyone loves to see you smile and hear you laugh, but it's up to you to decide that you love it too.

In Spite of You

You are so simple.
Ain't you tired?
Aren't you tired?
So you just gonna stand right over there and act like you don't see me?
OK.
If that's the game we're playing…
OK.
You are so simple.
The thing is, I already know how it's gonna go down.
You'll eventually get so close that you can smell my breath, then say,
"Oh—hi, Jaaaaaz!! How are you?? It's so good to see you!!"
Smiling like a politician on the campaign trail.
With your fake ass.
Why you mad?
Why you gotta be upset with me?
Got your lips poked out 'cause I got a little bit of recognition.
'Cause I can put one foot in front of the other without your help.
Because I can get from Point A to Point B without asking you for directions.
You're upset with me because you're not going anywhere, and you act like I'm holding you back.
All you have to do is put the keys in your ignition and go!
You might surprise yourself.

But I guess until then, you'll be angry, and we'll play this game.
Seriously?
I'm walking around with this orange mop on my head—who can miss that??
It's cool, though…
'Cause while you're standing over there, I'm staring a hole in the back of your head, and I'm happy.
Because my Ferrari is outside running right now, ready to take me from zero to sixty in 2.3 seconds.
C. Blount said I'm a poet 'cause I don't have the guts to tell you to your face.

Aye! Aye! I'm tapping you on your shoulder 'cause I need you to read my lips.

In spite of you—I go.
In spite of you— do.
In spite of you—I grind.
In spite of you—I succeed.
In spite of you—I am.

• • •

A Closer Look: "In Spite of You"

It was a lonely day when I realized that not all my friends were excited to see me succeed. In all honesty, I couldn't comprehend why any of my buddies, close friends, colleagues, or associates put on sour faces when they learned of my accomplishments. I just couldn't understand. Early on, I took it personally and it hurt my feelings. How could it not? Someone I thought was on my side all of a sudden appeared to be anything but. Dare I even say "hating" on me? Ouch. That's behavior you expect from an enemy or a not-so-good friend, but definitely not from someone you thought had your back. But it happens and it happens a lot, and it's gonna hurt my fingers to continue writing this narrative, but I've got to do it. Just know that if you've ever experienced this or anything close to it, you're not alone.

Before I dig in, let's be clear that as I write, I'm not in any way talking about all of your friends. I'm only talking about those special few whose colors seemed to change over the course of time. Here's the deal: they're excited for you as long as you're not doing better than they are. There—I said it. They will high-five you, pat you on the back, and congratulate you as long as you've not eclipsed them too badly in this marathon of life. They'll even throw you a party if you surpass them a bit, as long as your coattails are still within arm's reach. But the moment you turn a lap, get your second wind, and start sprinting like there's no tomorrow, you can almost kiss your buddy goodbye. You've left them; they feel like they'll never be able to catch up, and now they want nothing to do with you. Your success, no matter how large or small, holds a mirror to their face, showing them who they could be and what they could have if only they worked hard enough…were dedicated enough…were focused enough…were determined enough…were disciplined enough. All of a sudden you've proven the impossible to be possible, and though it appears so, they're not actually upset with you—they're angry with themselves. These were hurdles they assumed you'd be jumping together, but you got ants in your pants and jumped the gun on a few of them, leaving your buddy behind. And what they fail to realize is that even though you're a few laps ahead, you've still got their back, you're still cheering them on, you still want to see them succeed, but they're too busy pouting to even see that. It's such a sad situation. Every year thousands drink hater-ade, and scores of friendships dissolve because of it. My advice to those who have lost a buddy or two along the way? Never stop making new friends. As you climb new towers and reach new heights, introduce yourself to the new bunch around you. They'll be excited to hear how you got there and they'll be ready to cheer you on to your next stepping stone, because they're headed in the same direction.

Nothing on Paper

I don't really have anything on paper.
No poem to recite…
So I'm just gonna speak from the heart if that's all right.
I don't know how you've been doing,
But I've been living in hell for some time now,
And I'm done feeling sorry for myself.
I'm done talking about the pain that you've inflicted on me.
Because, bottom line: you couldn't have done it without my permission.
For whatever reason I laid down and let you clean the soles of your shoes on the backs of my shirts.
But today I've decided to do laundry.
Because whether you know it or not—
Whether you can see it or not—
Whether you give a damn or not—
I'm worth more than that.
I'm tired of wearing this filthy shirt so I'm reaching for my Clorox bleach
To wipe away every memory and leave me with a clean slate.
A new beginning—
A new day—
A new era—
Because I love myself.
Because I possess seeds of greatness that must be planted.

Because I've got my own back.
Because I'm not weak.
Because even in my silence I'm larger than life.
Because I'm on a mission.
Because you don't have to understand.
Because I'm hungry.
Because I'm starving.
Because I'm thirsty.
Because following my dreams is my balanced meal.
Because time is of the essence.
That's it.
And I hope you can forgive me,
But this is the kind of shit you end up saying when you have nothing on paper.

• • •

A Closer Look:
"Nothing on Paper"

Let's just be honest. Sometimes you need to vent. Sure, there are those who take it upon themselves to let the world know how they're doing every second of the day, but on the flip side, you've got folks who hold it all in (I'm in that basket). You never want to be viewed as the Complainer, so you say nothing. You'd rather drive your bleeding self to the emergency room than burden someone else with your troubles. You'd rather be homeless than ask for a handout. You know who you are. I can't even say that there's anything inherently wrong with that kind of behavior, but I've got a few tips for people who are sitting on both sides of the fence.

First, to those who tend to hold it all in and deal with everything on your own—open up. Not to everyone, but to someone. Certainly there's at least one person you trust deeply, and if there isn't, well, that's an entirely new can of worms to be dealt with at another time. Harboring stress has such negative effects on your physical, mental, and emotional health. When you look at the facts, it really isn't worth it. There is only so much pressure a person or a thing can take before breaking, and you want to avoid your breaking point at all costs. So confide in someone, because guess what? You're actually empowering your confidante when doing so. Let me show you what I mean. When you remain bottled up, your closest pals feel helpless. In their eyes you've got the strength of ten mountains, and they feel as if there's nothing they can do for you. And because of the type of person you are, I'm guessing you do for them all the time. They're probably always leaning on you for one thing or another and you're always there. Let me let you in on something—they're dying to return the favor, but you never give them the chance. Allow them the opportunity to show you that same kindness. And what you'll find is they won't judge you, and opening up won't sting nearly as bad as you anticipated it would.

Now to the friends of the "bottled up." Please take a moment to put yourselves in their moccasins. From the outside looking in, your friend appears to be a pillar of strength. They always make the right decisions...they're logical thinkers and planners...if there's a job that needs to be done, they do it. No matter how difficult the task seems, they dig in without hesitation, and you love that about them. They're always dependable, reliable, and super trustworthy. Do you have their moccasins on yet? What I need you to realize is that behavior and those characteristics you so love in your friend weren't developed overnight, and they require a lot of work to maintain. Think about the person who's always in a good mood—that's work! The person who never seems to get upset—that's work! And the same goes for your friend. Trust me, it takes a lot of effort to be the kind of person others can lean on. No doubt it's rewarding, but it's work nonetheless. So my request to you is cut your dependable, always-there-for-you friend a little slack. When you go to them for help and advice, don't leave the conversation without asking them how they're doing. It would even be a nice gesture for you to reach out to them every once in a while just because. When people are perceived as strong, outsiders fail to realize that even these strong individuals need some TLC every once in a while. And if you deliver, don't be surprised if your bottled-up pal becomes more of an open book.

Still Standing

like a stone wall.
like a steal beam.
as a sidewalk is long.
I'm strong.

like the mountains high.
like the redwoods.
like a gospel song.
I'm strong.

like a premature baby.
like a young single mother.
standing for right, not wrong.
I'm strong.

when the wind blows.
when the rocks are thrown.
i will not be gone.
I'm strong.

• • •

A Closer Look: "Still Standing"

Let's face it. Nothing is perfect 100 percent of the time. No matter what you wish for and no matter how hard you try to avoid them, tumultuous times will fall upon you. They make you feel like you're swimming in chaos, or like you're drowning in an avalanche while battling the Abominable Snowman. Your life appears to have become one big, disorganized free-for-all. Nothing is working the way it should. None of your plans fall into place. You keep missing the targets you've set for yourself, and slowly you begin to doubt if you even have what it takes to get the job done. But of course you've got what it takes. These crazy times have clouded your vision for the moment, and you've got to figure out how to regain your twenty-twenty.

Let me talk about physical health for a second. You know it's always easier and better to prevent an ailment than it is to treat it. Preventative care, it's called. Supplements, exercise, and tailored diets are all a part of preventative medicine. These are the things you do to stave off the ugly stuff. You may quit smoking in hopes of preventing lung cancer, or stop drinking to save your kidneys. You might add a bit of yogurt or a calcium supplement to your diet to keep your bones strong. And the list goes on. There is no shortage of things that people are doing to keep themselves in the best possible physical health, and I would argue that your mental health should be just as important to you.

What's mental health got to do with it? Well, when all hell breaks loose in your life, unless you were involved in an accident of some kind, you generally don't take a physical beating—your mind takes the beating for you. You get frazzled and you begin to lose confidence in yourself. And when you don't believe in you, you're in bad shape. You can definitely try to deal with the disarray when it happens, but my suggestion is preventative care. You don't know if you will ever have to battle a major sickness or disease, but you know there is no escaping difficult times. Hardships, depression, career setbacks, and financial challenges are just a few of the uglies that hop on your back from time to time. And though the preventative care I'm about to suggest won't prevent them, I do believe it will keep you ahead of the game in such a way that the ugly situation stings a lot less than it typically would.

So let's talk. What are those things that cheer you up when you're in a slump? Hanging out with friends? Listening to a certain kind of music? Watching comedic movies and shows? Laughing your head off in general? Working out? Running? Dancing like nobody's watching? Playing with your kids (or with somebody else's)? Cooking? Arts and crafts? Only you know those things that you can count on to bring you genuine happiness. My suggestion is that you don't wait for the storm to come. Find a way to incorporate these things into your daily lives—daily. Yes, daily. Just the same way that you might take your multivitamin every day, I'm asking you to find a way to laugh every day. Or carve out some time to play with the kids every day. Work on your arts and crafts daily. Whatever your "thing" is, find a way to get a taste of it each and every day, because this is what you'll find: the next time ugliness lands on your doorstep, no matter how devastating the situation is, it won't rattle your cage nearly as bad. By taking your daily dose of fun, you've banked all this positive energy, and now you have a place to use it. Even though you didn't know the ugliness was coming, you seemed ready for it. It tried to knock you down, but it couldn't. Now you're able to wave your fist to the universe and shout, "Is that all you got? Hahaha! I'm still standing!"

Final Thoughts

That's it. You've read some of my innermost thoughts and emotions. My hope is that you found something that spoke to you in a special way, something that fed your soul. If there's something that you're currently wrestling with, something that seems to be overtaking your life in a negative way, know that you're not alone, and know that daylight always comes after darkness. Oftentimes, in order to appreciate the best, we have to experience the worst, but it's only temporary. In the grand scheme of things, it won't matter, because we possess seeds of greatness that have been charged to produce an abundance of deliciously ripe fruit. So you've got one homework assignment from me: stop crying over the milk that has spilled and get ready to receive your harvest, because your time is coming. After the wind stops blowing and once the dust has settled, I will be right there with you, and we will be *Still Standing*.

www.ingramcontent.com/pod-product-compliance
Lightning Source LLC
Chambersburg PA
CBHW070134100426
42744CB00009B/1831